TODDLER WORDS BOOK

Colors Picture Cards For First 100 Simple Kids Words

RHODA RIN

Copyright2017 By : Rhoda Rin.
All rights reserved.No part of this book
May be used or reproduced in any matter
Whatsoever, without permission in writing
From the author, except in the case of brief
Quotation embodied in critical articles or review.

Lion

Tiger

Black Bear

Giraffe

Cheetah

Panda Bear

Grizzly Bear

Lemur

Elephant

Koala

Seal

Deer

Zebra

Hippo **Rhino**

Tortoise **Frog**

Snail

Penguin

Camel

Crocodile

Polar Bear

Potato

Carrot

Peas

Cabbage

Pepper

Aubergine

Broccoli

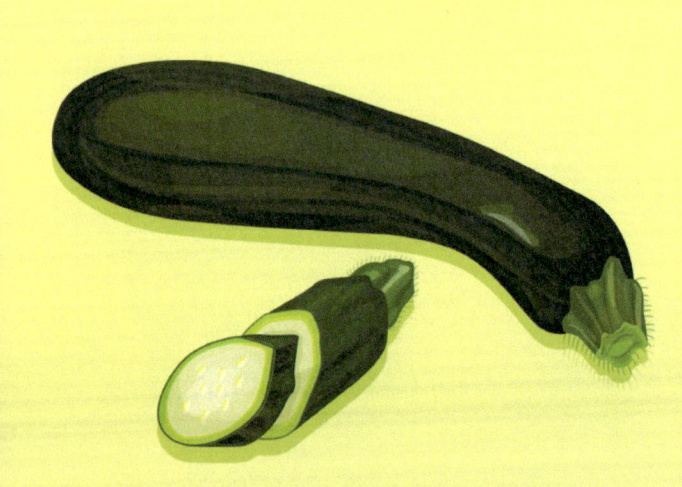

Courgettes # Cucumber

Mushroom

Leeks

Corn

Onion

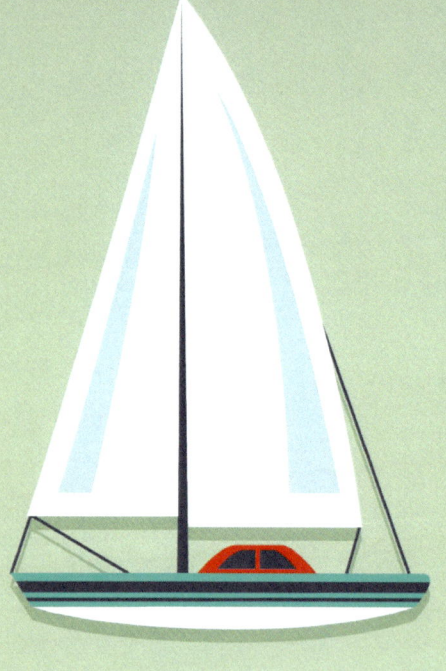

Boat

Ship

Car

Bus

Motorbike

Bike

Train

Helicopter

Van

Lorry

Underground

Plane

Hot air balloon

Cararan

Jeep

Submarine

Robot

Marbles

Crayons

Teddy

Puzzle

Football

Bricks

Board game

Camera

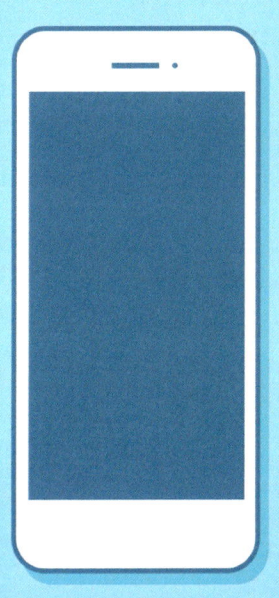
Mobile phone

Mouse

Kite

Computer

Keyboard

Plug

Light switch

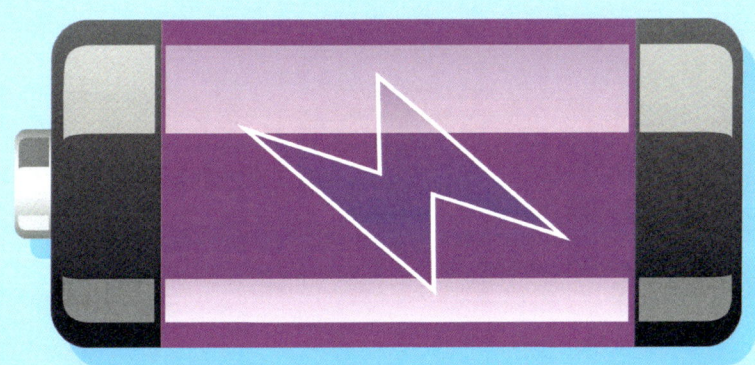
Batteries

Helmet

Racquet

Scooter

Hockey stick

Goggles

Sun

Moon

Stars

Earth

Planet

Rocket

Comet

Asteroid

Flying saucer

Alien

Octopus

Seahorse

Angel fish

Crab

Whale

Dolphin

Shark

Lobster **Tuna**

Coral **Shell**

Starfish

Squid

Jellyfish

Made in the USA
Columbia, SC
10 December 2018